A HORSE MADE OF FIRE

poems

HEATHER BELL

COBALT PRESS
Baltimore, MD

Copyright © 2015
ISBN: 978-1-941462-08-9
Cover design by Amanda Ponder
Book design by Andrew Keating

Cobalt Press
Baltimore, MD

cobaltreview.com/cobalt-press

All rights reserved. No part of this book may be reproduced in any form, except for the inclusion of brief quotations in review, without written permission from the author/publisher.

For all inquiries, including requests for review materials, please contact cobalt@cobaltreview.com.

A HORSE MADE OF FIRE

3	I Don't Use Them Anymore
5	Your Hands in So Many Similes
7	What to Do If Someone You Love is Dead
9	LOST
11	I Start to Drink
13	Conversation with Allison
15	When the World Does Not Come Easily
17	Funeral Shoes
19	Heartbreaker
21	And If You are Sad Enough
23	In the Clinic Parking Lot
25	And I Bury
27	Wakened Body
29	I Thought of My Life
31	Decoding the Poem
33	I Know that I Have Died
35	Letter, Unfinished, Come Back
37	Last Will and Testament
39	Quick Thinking
41	What Do I Teach My Daughter About Poetry
43	The Sweater

A HORSE MADE OF FIRE

45	April 02 2011
47	This is the Thing I Will Never Tell My Daughter
49	For Her Unborn Son
51	Girl with Monkey's Heart Writes
53	Matryoshka, Nesting Doll
55	Not a Poem About Anything in Particular
57	Sewn
59	The Beginning
61	Umbrella
63	Executioner
65	A Love Poem During Marriage
67	You, Her Mother, Her Child

For Jerrad

A HORSE MADE OF FIRE

A HORSE MADE OF FIRE

I Don't Use Them Anymore

"The trains. I don't use them anymore," he said
to me, one eyebrow a little more rambunctious than
the other. "We are in this world to be swept away,"
he said. We were playing around in the ocean,
our families rented a cottage for the week, summer
vacation. He was eleven. His father was wearing
a sweatshirt with the sleeves cut off and smoking
and swearing about the lack of Asian hookers

here on Millbrook Island. His father taught me
to be afraid of serial killers. Once, after a
particularly scary movie, he hid in my closet and
ran out holding a kitchen knife. I had just been
undressing. He started laughing. His father also

gave me this fear of men. "How old were you
when you knew you were a lesbian?" asked Paul,
the eleven year old boy, wearing nothing but his
underpants, holding a plastic cup, letting the water
in and letting the water out. In and out. Years
later I begin to question whether tragedy makes us
philosophers or philosophers give us
stories of tragedy and we insert them into our lives.

Little Paul, he asks whether his father ever touched
me in the hymn. I think, years later, he must have
meant *hymen*. His father used to call me Girl of Sweet
Words. He saw me undressing, he laughed, shook his
head and said, "maybe when you have something to
show me, I'll come back." Little Paul tells me the best
part about waves is that they can't leave you. Years
later, I am touching another woman as if she is

4

A

H
O
R
S
E

M
A
D
E

O
F

F
I
R
E

the too far between the man ripping off your pants
and your leg and his scrotum. Little Paul waves his
hands in front of my face to alert me that his father
is coming, seems happy, is holding something in his
arms like a child. It is a large bone, big enough to be
an elephant's. I have often wondered if bones have
cores, says Paul. As if you can break it and inside

there are seeds to make new people. Or new
bones. His father waves the bone around and
asked us if we might know where a bone like this
comes from. I say, "it's mine," and I take it
and I run.

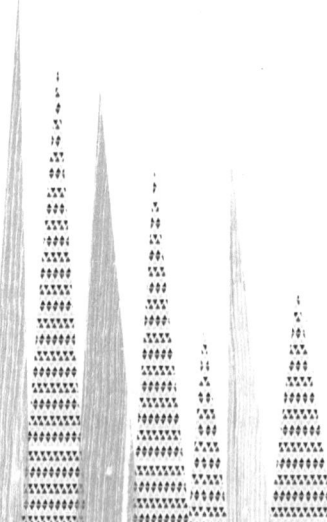

Your Hands in So Many Similes

Like the warm water in September. Like the scabs, the fence wire at KZ Herzogenbusch. Like 60 species of wildlife on your front lawn and standing there thinking, *beautiful, but how?* Like the flags of skin left on my toes after a 10-mile hike through the desert. Like the grass looking up in the morning waiting for dew or sprinklers or waiting for you to sob again. Like the long history of our ancestors raping women, holding women, beating their children to death.

Like a Klansman's hood. Like writing a chain song and every detail is true and every sentence is a bastard holding a saxophone. Like *ego amo te*. Like *es milu tevi*. Like *tave myliu*. Like sitting in an ash tree outside of my house and calling down these things, these predatory root words. Like wearing orange slippers while your father confesses his homosexuality. Like something wild slicing through the trees. Like Andrea Yates, pushing her babies heads under in the bathtub. Like saying, "nothing is going to last." Like falling asleep during *Brokeback Mountain* and waking up to your best friend crying, her head turned away. Like eating the green tops of carrots while you're pregnant, eating sweet cakes, the planet of your body sometimes sitting in the backyard and stuffing its mouth full of paper and clay. Like your high school janitor found in the art room in a transvestite's sharp mascara and rouged cheeks. Like almost shooting your .22, it could have been your father, it could have been your therapist, but it was just a nocturnal animal nosing its face through the brush. Like guinea pigs or are they people? Like waking up at

3am full of tears and death and death. Like death. Like waking up at 3am, full of the knowledge that life is finite. Like killing bees or killer bees. Like waking up at 3am, feeling your body as it is, a burden. Like your fingers touching my hip lightly as if you feel the same way. Like *we regret to inform you* taped to your door. Like 3am. Like 3am and you are touching my hip lightly. Like asking people for their death stories, thinking theirs may negate yours. Like lilies and moss and mountain lion. Like it is 3am, I am not sleeping, you are not touching my hip lightly as if to say, *I will always be here.* Like *konoronhkwa.* Like *kocham ciebie.* Like wondering what you are talking about and then crying again, it doesn't matter. Like being held, there you are.

Like 3am, you're here. Like you, saying "*ja tebe koKHAju*" over and over again, as if repetition makes it true. Like a dead deer at the end of the road, dead-end, how ironic. Like you, 3am, telling me a story about a woman getting an electrocardiogram. Like the way they told the woman to please be still to get an accurate read. Like please be still, be still. Like the way I am held, legs to my chest, covered in a blanket like a baby might be, somewhere in the world. Like reaching for you, walking hand over hand like an ape. Like saying, "*Ani ohevet otcha.*" Like you, laughing, nodding. Like 3am and yes and yes and holding me and yes.

H
E
A
T
H
E
R

B
E
L
L

G

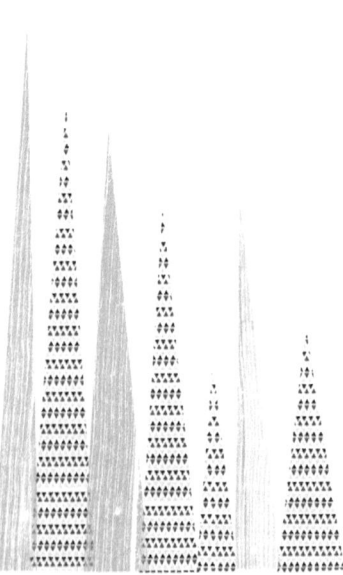

WHAT TO DO IF SOMEONE YOU LOVE IS DEAD

I ask a lot of people about death, as if their death stories may
negate my own. The man at the park, he says she just "keeled
over and died." He cries a little. Overhead there is darkness
and a reddish cloud, as if his grief is so heavy to bear that the
sky cannot hold it in. My mother telephones me, "I never
meant for us to never speak again." There is a trail of blue

hats from my house to the street and I make bad coffee like we
live in Alcatraz. My husband calls me *killer* because I get

things done, and I call him *Jerry Lewis* because he seems
to be rotting but is very optimistic about it. I tell my best
friend about a book I read recently, all the babies died and
the mothers did not care. It was as though morning was

night and all the world had a backside we wanted to
spank and cry and spank and cry and swear we don't
normally do things like this but just this once you deserve
it, world. I listen to the little feet of rain on the roof.

Jennifer comes over. We chat about turkey and wild rice,
tiger lilies, vacations to Delhi. She tells me her father died

on this day, years ago. That with a little crumbled bacon,
the turkey from last week can still be good to eat. That
perhaps it is best to get as far away from here as possible.

My husband returns to me as if he is returning from a long
trip. He crawls into bed and he is no longer my husband,
but an investment banker or accountant. This makes it

easier to talk about nothing. I return to the doctors and
they take my blood, O-negative. They tell me I could probably make
a lot of money off of blood like mine. I laugh a little, I say
"take it." I have nowhere else to go.

Lost

He finds me sitting in the backyard. I say,
"I lost the baby." I tell him I have been
putting up flyers all afternoon as if I lost
a Llasa Apso. I touch my husband's

thorax, there, in the garden. I touch
his wings and mouthparts.

I wrote on the flyer,
next to a photograph of a little girl I found,
Laney Davenport, found dead in a river
last week, according to the newspaper:

LOST: someone who loves you.
The wet pit inside all larger fruits.
An escapee from the state prison.
Bleeding out parts of ourselves, not
yet girl or boy, not yet dragonflies.
Boat oil to keep boats running, not
hitting the reef and everyone dies.

With a sense of history, my husband
touches me, pulls me back inside
and into the bedroom, to our
sickbed. It feels too low to the

ground, as if I am a Moroccan
woman, kind of sleeping but also
must still be half awake, shell the

crab steaks laying next to me on
the dirt floor. My hands moving
up and over and up and over

even when I can sneak real
dreams. Grabbing for something.

LOST: heart in the shape of a
peony. Small, inconsequential.
Might be in your backyard pool.
Might be doing the dead man's float.

I Start to Drink

When you had not returned, and it was 6am,
I started to drink. And it was not just the old
liquor that started me into thinking I might

want to have an affair, but the tap water
and the dog water, too. I drank up the woman's
red hair in the dish at the sink. I pureed

butcher's paper, the impotent balls of
a mouse, one wing pulled from a horse
fly. I choked down the hard bits of

potato soup that you left at the table,
your saliva hanging at the bowl's lip.

When you had not returned and it was 8am,
my mouth was a crow, my arms were crows,
my legs were crows, and we were a murder,

together. I drank the condolences
from my mother, as if you were already
dead. I sat on my haunches and I telephoned

the operator and spoke low and breathy
as if the operator might want to have sex
with me. I sat on my roof, wine glass in

my hand, thinking of catching all
free things, putting them in my blender,
setting it on high. I watched a couple

of birds do acrobatics over my house.
I wondered what the world
looks like to them from up there:

12 A HORSE MADE OF FIRE

the way wind makes you cry a
little so everything looks wet.
The way you have to keep moving
in order not to break your body
open. The way it must look

beautiful, but always tilted,
just slightly, as if it is about to
roll away.

Conversation with Allison

"It just was what it was," she said.
I had not disappeared or
floated off with a million other small leaves,

but that was how it seemed to my husband
at the time.

And you know, she told me, you could
not have found me on a map

once I was gone. A woman does not

have coordinates or North and South
etched into their body, as men seem

to think.

She laughs.

Maybe I will become a lesbian, or,
something just as beautiful—the woman

wearing a turquoise necklace next
to you in line at the grocery store,
popping her knuckles, unworried,

passing the time as if it were
a road hazard.

At some point (she touches the flowery
bits of her hair as she speaks) he

had to realize that rage was not
my happiness backwards. I kept thinking
that—at some point he will realize.

How silly of us, I suppose, to believe
a man wants us for more than a socket
to screw into.

She laughs, eats an edge of sandwich.

The point is, if you close your eyes and
press hard on them, you begin to see
flashes of lightning, a currant color,

and some people think you can
predict your future like this. But I

used to try it and it just made me tired.
I would loosen my hands eventually and
wake up five hours later, dishes in the sink,
my mouth sore like I had been
biting down on something for years.

When the World Does Not Come Easily

When the world does not come
easily, we find blue feathers in our

backyards and we make houses

out of these feathers and these feathers

blow away with just a light wind, as
we knew they would. "I'm not trying to be

profound or poetic by saying these
things," I told my husband. "I just

thought that they were the right words
and eventually you would figure it

out." I could not say *terror* or

new species of love so I said

what I could say. I could not say *stop*

or *why*, so instead we argued
for hours about feathers. Feathers.

There was an ugly little bird I found
dead in my yard yesterday, which I did not bury,
but picked up and threw into our
trash bin. In your bird book, it calls him

a blackcap. I always thought
sadness was like that, a black helmet
or dog pelt over your head. I felt

16   so sorry after that, dug him out of
     the garbage, and covered him in blue
A   tissue paper. I left him in your briefcase,
     beak pointed up and open as though
H   he was about to speak.
O
R
S
E

M
A
D
E

O
F

F
I
R
E

Funeral Shoes

The red ones. Five-inch stilettos, otter- or beaver-skin
lined. I can never remember. Human-skin lined. If you
look close, atoms at the heel. Palpitations at the heel.

I can never remember. Baby Ollie is dead, little elephant
tongue in his felt shoes. Aunt Marybeth, carved bone
over the knee boots. Nightmares stitched in the toe.
Beer in the toe. I can never remember. The red ones,

voicemail in their curves. Hello, I can never remember
your name, but your mother is dead. Your daughter
is on a smoke break, November 18th, nail popped through

a slipper. Quiet, quiet, she's sitting outside on your front
stoop, can you let her in? I can never remember, the workmen

at her feet like slaves. Is this the way *I am sorry* feels
to most animals? Sealskin at the tip, a little blood still
around the ankle.

H
E
A
T
H
E
R

B
E
L
L

Heartbreaker

My father doesn't wake up. I laugh because laughter is a nest
sometimes. A place to wring our hands. A place to set down

into the Red Sea, use your body as a boat, hair as anchor.

At thirteen years old, my father challenges me to use
poltergeist in a poem in place of *heart*,

which I used too often. At the time, I turned away,
started smoking cigarettes with my best friend,
began planning my escape. And now, I cross to the window,

listen to the quiet loon of machinery, touch the little plastic
cup sitting there like a taxidermy. I begin to

wonder what the dead think of that which we have not
done nor will ever do. Are we still such failures or

do they look into us now as we peer into refrigerators,

feeling hunger, and can only wish silently for
chocolate cake or new milk. I walk to him, touch

his chest bandages like cut flowers and
I recall a poem he read to me once in which a

beautiful woman says yes and yes and yes,
but the man has no heart left
to love with.

And If You are Sad Enough

And if indeed you are sad enough—
if your backache feels like it has a tiny
broken heart—
if your topography of sadness is littered with
your mother's tired feet
and your father's poison oak-

if you have found your natural home
is a handful of caught white fish-
if the scent of the earth
is body and cave—

now is the time to stock up
on canned goods like a
survivor. To place foliage in your hat
to fool the animals. Now

is the time to take your grandfather's
ventilator and attach it to your
throat to give
breath where there is none.

Now, take your rage and your
scarlet fever. Take your beautiful piano

and transplanted pig's
heart and place them all

in a basket. And if indeed you are sad enough,

push this basket far down
a river as if it were food moving
slowly past the teeth, and

if you are sad enough,
you will hear it cry, quietly,
and suck greedily
on its fingers.

In the Clinic Parking Lot

Because you're just an embryo,
this might not make sense, but
bear with me:

there was a time in my life when
I went down to the pond and
there were hurt fish everywhere
on the land and I thought

oh what have we done
and we decided to buy new fish
and wept and whispered bees
into our own ears

and because you have not yet
lost your death and there is
pollen at your head top
you may not understand

but you need to know that
when I was a girl there was a wolf
sighting by the canyon
and I saw a deer spit venom into

the wolf's eyes and bite
the wolf at the ankle and

it wasn't until years later that
I met your father and tonight

I opened my old books and
bits of moth and hair were
clinging to the pages and

24 this world is absurd
and enormous and
A welcome.

H
O
R
S
E

M
A
D
E

O
F

F
I
R
E

And I Bury

I bury your heart like a placenta
in the backyard. I leave your
sadness in the driveway like
a midnight-foal. From the remains

of your coffee this morning,
I make all things go away:

the bitter, the hard swallow,
the skin at the edge of the
night. And the note I leave

is my discovery that NASA
uses Sanskrit to communicate

with extra terrestrials and
ancient people had a word for

here, which does not sound
anything at all like
here
or even
home.

H
E
A
T
H
E
R

B
E
L
L

Wakened Body

When I was thirteen years old, my mother changed her name to
Wakened Body. She began locking herself in her bedroom for days and
referring to my schooling as "The Great Depression." I remember
that I loved her best then, in the beautiful mauve skirt patterned
in open windows. It wasn't until I was in my twenties that she again

changed her name, this time to Shattered Universe (though she
could not tell me this at first). My father spent most of the time
drunk, pissing in the corner with his friends, or taking my homework

to the bathroom with a marker and spelling out *ZERO* all over the
page. I worked hard for each word for years, in order to tell
this story in a way that makes sense—my mother sitting so still

in the kitchen, hair cut short, skin gray, bag of something poisonous
at her elbow. "I am going to kill him tonight," she whispers and
perhaps think I can't hear. And the next thing I know,

he is asleep with pork around his beard and I press my head
to his chest and there are miles and miles of foot indentations

and years of planets and breath left, and my mother feeds the
bag's entrails to our dog, which only gives him diarrhea, and I am

so disappointed, thinking that if she was still Wakened Body,
she could have done it and she would go to bed tonight
without walking carefully past my father, throwing a galaxy
of blankets over the stove fire, putting it safely and finally
out.

I Thought of My Life

I thought of my life—that up
until now it was as if I had been handed

a rope, an engine and
a ripe apple and told

go, do—and instead I

became furniture,
ruffle around the legs like
an old bed.

I thought of my life—that the sound
of a person's wails can reach

the moon faster than
an astronaut. That I saw myself

as a med school diagram—

no sign of bruising, no
visible cuts.

I thought of my life—the siege we place
on the kitchen table
like soup every morning

as we get older and the belt I wear and
secretly tighten like a warrior.

I thought of my life—and then
I thought of you, without one memory of

being a crocodile
or cannibal
yet, and I want to ask you to think

of your life after you read this
and face the guns and
pull the arrow slowly
and carefully

from your hair.

Decoding the Poem

And the cardinal is December. And in December
there was blood and a wavering light. You describe
a flock of wild hair and it is that hair that makes me
keep still. I hold the phrase white tissue with my fingers
as if it is very small and broken. And there, I see

that you want me to touch a thing more dense
than air, but I know that you cry when you write
your letters, and the lack of stars

does not mean you are lonely, but only
that you are very alone, in that moment.

And there you place moodiness and there
you set grief, just as we did,

at the kitchen table
after you lost the baby. And there it is again—
December. And as always, December

is put there sneakily to make me think
that a staircase is a door, but I know you,

and this door is a hole
or wound that you walk through.

I Know That I Have Died

And I am in the emergency room and there is a woman
with a face of leaves. She calls me Precious Stone
and it is not until that moment that I know for sure

that I am dead. Because everyone is beautiful—

where are the tumored, the Socialists, the people
constantly reminding me of my own
failure? Because everyone is happy—

no bloody stumped men playing their
Church organs, no weeping women in
big hats. And I touch this woman's hand

and I ask *how long
have I been dead?* And she laughs,
each leaf going yellow and
rigid, and I know then
that I have been lied to

my whole sorry life, and she says
I looked like someone she knew,
just for a moment,
but she must have been mistaken.

Letter, Unfinished, Come Back

Because I backspace backspace
Dear include-interesting-pet-name-later,

This isn't what I expected it to be
delete
my pulse
exclamation point
mailman, sadness, isokinetic, period of twelve minutes
in which I write nothing,

Google *moon* at some point,
but the description is
not beautiful enough

Things that remind me of you:
forecast: rain, rain, typhoon,
more rain

include a photo
question mark

Finally something worth
saying—

last Thursday,
your head is a vowel,
owl or arm

start new paragraph
dear something-polite,

this is a way to describe the world-

start over

Last Will and Testament

In the event of my death,
no autopsy. I am embarrassed of most
of my internal parts. Mosquito-sized
heart, Civil War meat digesting, blood

crawling forward. Please donate
my mother to a hostel in Brazil.
Please take that which is not visible

but scented of flowers and bottle it,
give it to Josiah. Return my car

to the mailman, return my bank account's
balance to the government, return

my bubbling over pots to
the landlord. I guess I will miss

all of you. At my funeral,

give Uncle Harold my left fingerprint,
to help him with his thieving and
romancing of underage girls.

Do not open the chest at the end
of my bed, it is full of

the years you spent
looking for yourself in a mirror
and found only a dead person.

My lawyer keeps a swallow in a cage in his
living room. It is wild and I have always
found this to be very cruel,
until this moment.

I am leaving you
because of Tuesday, you remember:

walking in on you at the sink,
pouring boric acid over a mouse you had
captured in a cup. That was my favorite mug,

you know, the one with the witty saying
about life on the side and now

I no longer feel comfortable using
it for coffee,
which has made me feel so hopeless
and tired.

H
E
A
T
H
E
R

B
E
L
L

Quick Thinking

Last week, I received a winter coat in the mail with
no return address. In these moments, it is best to think
quickly—the color of a blot or boulder. The wonky zipper
that catches by the belly. The note in the pocket, just

aviary, and nothing else but an old thimble and
stain. And it fits, a bit too large, but I know that this

winter, it will do as well as anything. And I again,

think quickly—the color of machinery, ash. Something dead
that filters down from something burning. And there is a scent

at the wrists, and it isn't until today that I remember
that the last place I smelled something so dark was

in the barn behind the house, broom in my hand,
whacking a wasp nest and wanting to die and not caring

that I had not eaten since yesterday, though the hunger

is like quick thinking—the color of old leaves vibrating
like alcoholics trying so desperately to hold on.

What Do I Teach My Daughter About Poetry

That it was violent? That it was a noose? That at seven
months pregnant with her, I had given it up because I was
so terrified of that change in the wind that always comes

with a new poem? Perhaps that poetry is a river
or air or that if you count through the rumbling

it will get further and further away (but always
return when you wish just to put your feet down

for once, on the beach). And it is then that I

start nesting, as they say: pans must be organized,
no bleach on the bottom shelves, and all books of poetry

locked up. The final step: to know I will never speak

of my years as a poet, because those words were so
dangerous, it seems now. That it is enough to see my

child's mouth open for the first time in June,
hear nothing come out, as it is with such a surprisingly

sharp intake of air, sudden and shocking.

And then the wail.

HEATHER BELL

The Sweater

As a child, I never thought beyond what my mother
had taught me, which was simple enough: no dirty shoes
in the kitchen, no smiling when there is no reason

to smile, and the big sweater she always wore was
also for when you were sick, its big pockets good

for toy mice and bits of cotton to comfort.

I remember sneaking her sweater one morning, not
sick, just mischievous perhaps, to run barefoot

to the pond edge and slink in, quietly. There were

those weird green dragonflies that sit on the
water top and the blue heron and the cat tails and

they all looked at me like wild survivors. I said,

"I know that look," and winked. They say that every

child has a moment in which they discover their parents

are the tooth fairy and their priest thinks he is God,

and I felt the pull of something taking me under, and

my mother's sweater felt like bricks, and I knew I deserved

this on some level for being a bad kid, but

I also suddenly realized that the sweater had always bunched
up at my mother's spine because it was like this—life was always

44 like this. And my head was swallowed up and I could see the

A weird green bugs still sitting on the water top and they still
  looked like survivors.

H
O
R
S
E

M
A
D
E

O
F

F
I
R
E

April 02 2011

And it broke my heart so I put these particles back.
And it broke my heart so I slipped on my chinchilla coat
with the blood at the ears. And it broke

the vase from August, a gift, filled with meditation and
get-over-it. And there is a little girl that I fear

I kept with the queer idea that she might never grow
legs. And it broke my heart to sit on the hill and look

up and you said you would be there to watch me, but instead

there was just your animatronic creation. And it feels

like phantom hands playing over my hair. And I carry

a purse shaped like a medicine cabinet. And the parts

fell off when I tried to pin it together and the buttons

also did not work and the snaps had a metal

grip that would not slot into
anything.

HEATHER BELL

This is the Thing I Will Never Tell My Daughter

This is the thing I will never tell my daughter:
that there were years that my own mother
did not love me. It is sad to know this

for sure. Because there were expectations:

law school, small house in the city,
a child and no man. But,

I kept your father like I kept
you, unable to give up on something that

seemed so small and fragile
at first. And because I told my mother

of my hunger strikes and deep
sadness and notions of what childhood
was not. Because that is what might

make one person give up on
another person: honesty. And through these years,

I watched my beautiful husband
try to get the grass to live easily

under the hundred-year-old pines and each
year he failed until

he found a book that told him of
a weird scientific mix of seed that can grow

even in the darkest parts
of a person's yard, and it was in that year

48 that I held you for the first time,
silent until

A

 the doctor suctioned your throat
H raw and clean.

O

R

S

E

M

A

D

E

O

F

F

I

R

E

For Her Unborn Son

It makes me sad for her unborn child—
that with his touch she will become madder

and madder and slowly strip to bits.

Just as we all do as mothers, but

this time will be different, as she started

where we normally end: the heart of a

moray eel, the skin of a postcard too long

in the mail, the clean and quick understanding

of an infomercial cleaver. It's not that I think

she would murder him, but that

I am very sorry for the floorboards on which
he will tiptoe when afraid,

only to be shooed back

to his monsters.

Girl with Monkey's Heart Writes

And in the event of a monkey's heart being replaced
with my own, please tell Cindy that

I sympathize with her reasons. I know how hard it is,
as a woman, not to take your anger

and twist it upwards, out of the mouth. How difficult

her life must be, waking with her hair dampened into
stringy anemones, eating the hard chocolate cake promised

to her son. The religion of her marriage moving her
life from country to city, the deep love gone

intergalactic, now residing on the moon. And I never intended

to write something like this: *I have always thought
she was beautiful, her hair combed and curled forward,*

so unintentionally white trash, I am saying so because

monkeys love what is around to be loved,
which is simple.

And, also, a monkey's artwork can end up in museums,
shit on canvas and

I think you know what I'm talking about.

Matryoshka, Nesting Doll

And in the world there was a crowd
and in the crowd there was one person
with red sacred hair and

all over her mouth was paint and all over her knuckles
were marks where you can tell she has been beating

something inside of something else. Perhaps pushing
a shadow onto a human or continually punching

farm-raised hearts into a man
hoping one would take.

And all over this woman there was hard waxy skin,
not like the sea at all,
as a woman should be and

inside of this woman's skin there was

another woman who has anchors for hands and
a metronome where her eyes should be

like a woman should,

keeping time waiting for
the crowd to catch up.

H
E
A
T
H
E
R

B
E
L
L

NOT A POEM ABOUT ANYTHING IN PARTICULAR

I'm not going to tell you about the bleeding half-dead chicken that I stuffed into a corner of our garage with the hope that you would not find it. I will not use this shameful thing as a metaphor for our love: that I just wished to finish that which you said I would not do- end something sharp and bright. And that halfway through bone, I became afraid of the crying and the next step:

to eat our dead or bury it. I will only lean to you in the evening like a tree in heavy wind and admit my smallness. That you were right about us: the past is just the past, easily forgotten. And I will not hear weeping for days behind the old car parts, and I will not hear sad scratching at the cement floor, as if it is possible to escape a prison with just a sharpened hairbrush or spoon.

Sewn

When she is seven months old, I start writing poems in secret.
Someday, I think, she will tear open her old giraffe and find a galaxy,
a gut punch. I sew up each stuffed toy, and hand it to her as if to say

this is something you need to chew on. And like any teething baby,
she puts my poems in her mouth. She senses Ollie the Octopus is different,

but is unsure why. And that is how I say

mommy hates herself sometimes, so here is a stuffed pink pony
and you will lose interest in it someday but

someday after that you will open it like my heart and realize
it is a horse made of fire.

The Beginning

As a child, there was one instance in which
I was given a communion dress. It was covered in
hysterical sharpie pictures: deer, headlights,
girl. My mother said, "I can wash that out."

So the little girl gave me the dress and as
she handed it over, I noticed her hands moved
as if she was packing a suitcase. But I was

seven years old and I didn't understand then

that the wingspan of a bird directly correlates
to the tips of a human's fingers
to their heart. And by that I mean,

that each anniversary my husband and I will someday
celebrate will be buttered in loss. That
we will kiss as if there are dead
children holding our heads back.

So my mother washes the dress: it is beautiful,
white, clean. The little girl comes over,
sees the dress, demands to have it back. Some adults

parent like vultures so her mother put out her
hands and I placed the dress there like
I was waiting for a bone to be set.

And the point of the story is never the middle or beginning,
but in what your mother says at the end, "that I was very
proud of you that day, you waited until they left
to cry." Twenty percent of pregnancy ends in loss,

60   which is what I meant to say, at the beginning.
      And it is Sunday and I am thinking of old stories

A   in hopes of not thinking of this.

H
O
R
S
E

M
A
D
E

O
F

F
I
R
E

Umbrella

my first job was at a burger joint
I spent a lot of time washing trays with bleach
rubbing the corners

whipping clipped fingernails
into the trash basket

I ended up in the emergency room thinking
about my dress that opened at the hem like
an umbrella and how
I had not worn it in
months

I was only sixteen and that bleach
had burned off all my fingerprints

A nurse
in a whisper
asked me if I had been doing anything
strange with my hands

The lining of that umbrella skirt was
a strange pattern that always reminded
me of lungs
like it was saying

this is the skirt that will keep you breathing

and the more I didn't wear it
the more bleach I would dump
into the industrial sinks

until it was one big vat of toxic
fire until every time I entered
a room there wasn't a quietness
for the dying and

I said no I just don't know how this could have happened
any of it
and there was a hush to the room like something deadly
sitting down like an osprey maybe or
father and I got up to leave thinking that the

doorknob couldn't be dusted by police to find me
I could go
I could do anything

H
E
A
T
H
E
R

B
E
L
L

Executioner

And the baby is dead but
we need lettuce in the house, maybe some bread
for morning toast so

I am at the store touching the potatoes at the spine,
the slim wrist of carrot. And the baby is dead so

this entitles humans to talk about their dog's death,
or gerbil. This means I am expected to sympathize at

their loss. Because all death becomes, somehow, equal

when a childless person hears of a baby's slow start and
quick giving up.

So here is a poem I have written while curled up behind
the cartons of juice at the supermarket. Because the

crushed apples on the floor in the produce section were
her ears and eyes. The skin was so raw from sadness

that I knelt there to watch for too long.

And your dog might be dead too but you did not have to
watch him fall from inside your body like pieces of bird.

Teeth to knees, I spread her deadness in the bathroom
like it is the ocean and she is a gift.

A Love Poem During Marriage

And then she took a series of photographs of her face
and hung each one upside down in the bathroom. Because that
is where it started. And she has not showered for days,
months. So as she steps into the wetness, her hair becomes soft
like a small possum and the tile around her is forest and

she is walking. And she comes to a well, moon looking down
sadly like a human. As if to say she would not have been able
to love a disabled baby. So she touches the edge of the well

and inside she sees her hands wrapped up in butcher paper.
Because she could not drive to the hospital fast enough,
the moon looks down and removes that which she no longer needs.

She feels ready to leave the house so perhaps if you peeked in
you would see a normal woman not crying in the shower.
You would see her ready her hands to touch other hands.
You would see her soap her body at the neck, and see

no wound there. But her husband is standing silent while
she is not crying at a deep well and he holds the towel as if

it were a rope and bucket to drag her out.

You, Her Mother, Her Child

And so she decides to stay. For now. But it wasn't for you,
her mother or her child. It was that there was more
to report. For the statistics: ten percent of men kill

themselves in the same way she was planning. For
the deer's lungs left at the pond's bank as if to say

but I still need this place to breathe. For the weight
of ocean gathered into a suitcase. Because there is

always time to kill yourself, but not always time to
wear this day proudly, fused in like antlers.

And so, she tells you she lives for you, her mother,
her child. And in that moment a heron lands

at her shoulders, knowing it is best to stay close
to those bits of food that hover too close
to the water's edge.

A HORSE MADE OF FIRE

Acknowledgements

I'd like to thank Nicholas Cage, Basement Jared, my tits, rape culture, hashtags, zombie chicken, and my angelic children for being such an inspiration. I'd like to acknowledge guns, America, Franzia white merlot and the fact that I don't have a wall on one part of my house. It's a really great view. Booze is important. People are important, until they're not. Cigars are pretty nice, if you're in Vegas. I'd like to salute my husband for being an all-around badass and putting up with me during the making of this book.

Special thanks to Andrew and Stacie for creating this divisive black hole of a book and Rhiannon Thorne for putting up with my incessant questions and helping this book be known. Tabitha Surface, CarlaJean Valuzzi and Carlene Kucharczyk, I thank you so much for choosing this galaxy of stars. Amanda Ponder: I am so glad you slipped into my brain to sort out how to design the cover. You were the glamourous cricket singing by my window.

This book was easy to write. I say that because for the most part, poetry is solitary and quick and painful. Just some human, typing away. I thank myself for surviving it. I thank my babies that never made it, this is for you. You will always be my children, no matter how long you lived.

And anyone ever that buys this book: you just leveled up with this purchase—congratulations.

PREVIOUS PUBLICATIONS FROM THIS COLLECTION

"LOST," *South Dakota Review*

"And If You Are Sad Enough," *Poets/Artists*

"Decoding the Poem," *MOJO*

"Executioner," *THREE MINUS ONE, Stories of love and loss*

About the Author

Heather Bell's work has been published in *Cobalt Review, Rattle, Ampersand, Poets/Artists, NEON* and many others. She was nominated for the 2009, 2010 and 2011 Pushcart Prize from *Rattle* and also won the New Letters 2009 Poetry Prize. Heather has also published four books. Any more details can be found by visiting **hrbell.wordpress.com**.

MORE TITLES FROM COBALT PRESS

Four Fathers: fiction and poetry ($15.00)
Dave Housley, BL Pawelek, Ben Tanzer, Tom Williams
Foreword by Greg Olear

Black Krim: a novel ($15.00)
Kate Wyer

How We Bury Our Dead: poetry ($14.00)
Jonathan Travelstead

Enter Your Initials for Record Keeping: essays ($16.00)
Brian Oliu
Featuring "player two" essays by xTx, Tyler Gobble, Barry Grass, Tessa Fontaine, Jason McCall, Colin Rafferty, and more.

Cobalt Review, Volume 3: 2014 ($12.00)

Thumbnail Magazine 6 ($10.00)
Guest edited by Aubrey Hirsch

Additional 2015-2016 titles to be announced.

For more information about Cobalt Press publications, including our quarterly and annual literary journals, visit cobaltreview.com/cobalt-press.

www.ingramcontent.com/pod-product-compliance
Lightning Source LLC
Chambersburg PA
CBHW021447080526
44588CB00009B/733